Animal Pie

Compiled by Pat Edwards

Acknowledgements

We are grateful to the following for permission to reproduce copyright material: The Bodley Head on behalf of Norman Hunter and Gerald Rose for the story 'The Mouse War' and illustrations from *Professor Branestawm's Mouse War* by Norman Hunter, illustrated by Gerald Rose; the author, Morris Lurie for his story 'Arlo the Dandy Lion' from *Arlo the Dandy Lion* (pub. Penguin Books). Pages 40-5 were written by David Jamieson.

We have been unable to trace the copyright holder in the song 'Tiddalik' by The Cat Team from *ABC Sing Together* (1982) and would appreciate any information that would enable us to do so.

We are grateful to the following for permission to reproduce photographs: Cambridge Evening News, page 44 above right; David Jamieson, pages 40, 41, 42, 43, 44, 45.

Illustrators, other than those acknowledged above, include: Loui Silvestro pp. 4-17; Rolf Heimann pp. 18-19; Linda Forss pp. 20-9; Mary Ann Hurley pp. 30-1; Peter Foster pp. 32-9; Dave Parkins pp. 40-5; Gaston Vanzet pp. 60-1; G.A.S.P.P. pp. 62-4.

CONTENTS

Arlo the Dandy Lion   *Morris Lurie*   4

Africa — home of the lion   18

The Grandmother and the Butternut Pumpkin
Pat Edwards   20

What's Aesop's story?   30

Hi there, Slowcoach!   *Pat Edwards*   32

Animal stars   40

The Mouse War   *Norman Hunter*   46

Tiddalik   60

Frog jokes   62

Words to croak   *Glossary*   63

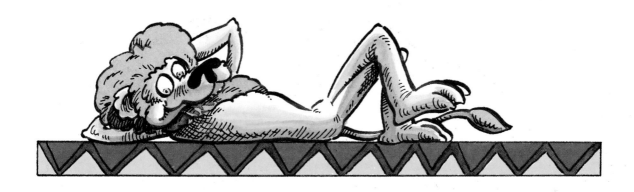

Arlo the Dandy Lion

There was once a young six-year-old lion named Arlo who looked like an ordinary young lion, but he wasn't.

He liked to leap like an ordinary lion, and he liked to roar like an ordinary lion, but the thing he liked to do best of all was to sit and study his reflection in ponds and pools, which is a thing ordinary lions never do.

"Stop being vain!" Arlo's brothers would say.

Arlo had four brothers who were all six, and who were all ordinary lions. Their names were Blake, Derrick, Benedict and Bob.

"Rrrrrrr!" Arlo would roar, studying his face in a pond or a pool. "I am a king of the beasts!"

"Silly Arlo," said his brothers.

One afternoon, Arlo found himself in a part of the jungle where he had never been before, and there, under a tall tree and almost hidden by long yellow grass, was a large red trunk.

"It must have been left here by explorers," said Arlo.

He opened the trunk, and the first thing he saw was a pair of yellow eyes.

Arlo blinked. The eyes blinked back.

5

"Help!" cried Arlo, and quickly jumped behind the tree.

But nothing happened, and after a while Arlo crept back to the trunk and had another look inside.

This time he saw a small black nose, a pair of soft yellow ears, some long shiny whiskers, a big mouth with a lot of teeth, and a young lion's shaggy mane.

"It's me!" cried Arlo. "It's a mirror! Just what I've always wanted!"

His heart beating with excitement, Arlo lifted the mirror out of the trunk and propped it up against the tree.

"It's better than looking in a pond or a pool," said Arlo, parading up and down in front of the mirror. "No ripples."

He bowed to his reflection, and then he smiled, showing all his teeth.

"I wonder what else is in the trunk?"

Back he went, and this is what he found.

There were hats (four), there were suits (eight), there were shirts (sixteen), there were handkerchiefs, scarves, socks, ties, and a pair of lavender-coloured braces. There were shoes (eight pairs), woolly jumpers (five), trousers (lots), jaunty jodhpurs, breezy shorts, a tweed jacket, an overcoat with a fur collar, a waistcoat with pearly buttons, a walking stick, and a box full of cuff-links and pins.

"A treasure!" cried Arlo.

He picked up the black bowler hat and tried it on for size. It fitted perfectly. He ran to the mirror to see how it looked.

"Very business-like," he said to his reflection. "Now, I wonder what goes with a black bowler hat?"

He put on a dazzling white shirt and a neat striped tie.

"Very nice," he said.

Next, he tried on a white linen suit, but that didn't seem quite right, so he tried a dark grey suit with a fine stripe in it.

"Perfect!" said Arlo.

He put on dark socks and shiny black shoes.

Then he picked up the silver-handled walking stick and gave it a twirl in front of the mirror.

"All I need now," said Arlo, "is a flower for my buttonhole," and he went to a nearby bush and plucked off a flower and tucked it into his lapel.

Then he went back to the mirror.

"Arlo," he said to his reflection. "You look magnificent. You must try on something else."

He tried on a dark blue suit.

Then a pair of shorts with a shirt all covered with flowers.

Then a red velvet suit with bright white buttons.

"Arlo," said Arlo, *"you are the best-dressed lion in all Africa."*

He was about to let out a roar when he thought, "No. A gentleman doesn't roar".

Just as he was deciding what to try on next, he noticed that it was growing dark. It was time to go home.

He had begun to take off the red velvet suit when he had an idea.

"I'm going home fully dressed," he decided. "Wait till my brothers see me like this!"

Very carefully, he folded all the clothes and put them back neatly inside the trunk. Then he fetched the mirror and put that back in too, and then he closed the lid.

Then, in his red velvet suit, Arlo started back through the jungle for home, twirling his silver-handled walking stick, smiling to himself and thinking how jealous his brothers would be when they saw him in his new clothes.

"Ridiculous!" said Blake.

"Outrageous!" said Derrick.

"Preposterous!" said Benedict.

"Silly Arlo!" said Bob.

Arlo was deeply hurt.

"You're only jealous," he said, and gave his silver-handled walking stick a twirl, just to show that he didn't care what his brothers said.

"Ha ha ha!" laughed Arlo's brothers.

Just then Arlo's mother came out of the kitchen where she was preparing supper.

"What's going on?" she said. "What's all that noise?"

And then she saw Arlo.

"Goodness!" she cried. "Arlo, you've fallen in the mud! Look at that nasty red stuff all over you! Go and have a bath at once!"

"It's not red mud," said Arlo. "It's a red velvet suit with bright white buttons."

"And what's that on your head?" cried Arlo's mother. "A bird's nest?"

"It is not a bird's nest," said Arlo. "It's a floppy hat."

"Oh dear!" said Arlo's mother. "What will your father say when he comes home and sees you like this?"

"I don't care what he says," said Arlo, brushing off some grass seeds which had got caught on his sleeve in the jungle. "I'm a gentleman."

"Oh dear!" said Arlo's mother.

Just then Arlo's father arrived. His name was Henry, and he had spent a pleasant day doing all the things lions like doing, namely, roaring full-throated deep-chested roars, stalking through the long grass, jumping from high rocks, swimming in the river, and, best of all, dozing in the cool shade of a leafy tree.

He was tired, and he was hungry, and when he saw Arlo in his red velvet suit with the bright white buttons, his mouth fell open.

"Good heavens!" he cried. "What's that?"

"It's me," said Arlo.

"What?" said Henry. "Why, so it is. For a moment I thought it was a man. What are you doing all dressed up like that?"

"Today," said Arlo, "I went into a part of the jungle I had never been in before, and I found a big trunk full of clothes. There were hats and shoes and socks and shirts and suits and – oh, lots of things!"

"Take that nonsense off at once!" Arlo's father roared. "You'll end up like your old Uncle Cecil. You'll end up in a zoo!"

"But Uncle Cecil didn't wear clothes," said Arlo.

"Take those clothes off at once!" roared Arlo's father.

"But I like them," said Arlo.

"Have you ever stopped to think," said Arlo's father, "why lions don't wear clothes? I'll tell you why. All lions are the same colour, that is, tawny, so they can blend into the trees and the grass and the rocks. But you, in that silly red suit, will be seen for miles and miles. What a terrible fate! Arlo, you have lost one of the lion's most prized possessions. You have lost the art of concealment."

"I don't care," said Arlo.

"You'll care," said Arlo's father. "Just you wait and see. Now, enough of this. Where's my supper? I've had a hard day."

"Silly Arlo," said Arlo's four brothers.

"You're only jealous," said Arlo, carefully hanging up his floppy hat.

That night Arlo dreamt of all the fine clothes in the big red trunk, and in the morning, as soon as he had eaten his breakfast, off he ran, back to his trunk under the tall tree.

He tried on all the shirts.

All the shoes and all the socks and all the ties and all the woolly jumpers.

"Arlo," said Arlo to his reflection in the mirror, "you are the best-dressed lion in all Africa."

That night Arlo went home wearing a purple jumper, a pair of grey shorts, long white socks and shiny black shoes, and the felt hat with the feather in the band.

"What?" said Arlo's father. "Are you still wearing all that nonsense?"

"Of course," said Arlo. "I'm the best-dressed lion in all Africa."

"Oh dear!" said Arlo's mother. "Arlo, you've fallen in the mud again!"

"I have not fallen in the mud," said Arlo. "These are new clothes. And tomorrow, I'm bringing home all my clothes, the whole trunkful."

And he did.

He put everything in his room, in the cave where the whole family lived.

"Excellent!" said Arlo to his reflection in the mirror, and out he went for a short stroll, twirling his walking stick.

First he passed a zebra.

"You look silly," said the zebra.

Then he passed a hippopotamus.

"You look ridiculous," said the hippopotamus.

Then he passed a monkey in a tree.

"You look foolish," said the monkey. "Why are you all dressed up like that?"

"I am the best-dressed lion in all Africa," said Arlo, and he strolled on.

15

After a while, he came to the bank of the local river and there he saw all his lion friends. Some were stalking in the grass, and some were swimming, and some were playfully wrestling, and some were dozing in the shade of leafy trees.

"Why, it's Arlo!" they said, when they saw him. "And he's wearing his funny clothes."

"Hello," said Arlo to his friends, twirling his walking stick. "Why are you wearing those funny clothes?" asked a lion named Clem.

"I am the best-dressed lion in all Africa," said Arlo.

"You'll end up in a zoo, all dressed up like that," said a lion named Bart.

"Nonsense!" said Arlo, and gave his walking stick another twirl.

"Come for a swim, Arlo," said Clem. "It's just what you need on a hot day like this."

"No, I don't think I will," said Arlo. "My clothes will get splashed."

"What about a friendly wrestle?" asked a lion named Oliver.

"No," said Arlo. "My clothes will get creased."

"What?" said Clem. "You don't want to swim or have a friendly wrestle? You're not a lion at all."

"I beg your pardon?" said Arlo.

"You're a dandy, not a lion," said Oliver.

"DANDY LION!" said a lion named David. "Arlo is a dandy!"

"DANDY LION! DANDY LION!" sang all of Arlo's friends. "DANDY LION! DANDY LION!"

"How rude they are," thought Arlo. He gave his walking stick a twirl and walked away.

Morris Lurie
illustrated by Loui Silvestro

Kilimanjaro

Madagascar

INDIAN OCEAN

Lake Victoria

Limpopo

Zaire

Zambesi

Kalahari Desert

Vaal

Orange

Cubango

SOUTH ATLANTIC OCEAN

Did you know?

- Lions do not live in the jungle. They are found on sandy plains, in rocky places where there are lots of thorn bushes, or in the tall, wild grass near waterholes.

- For the first few months of their lives, lion cubs are spotted.

- A fully grown lion can jump 3.8 m high and run at a speed of up to 80 km an hour.

The Grandmother and the Butternut Pumpkin

A play from Iran

Cast

Grandmother   **Wolf**

Tiger

Lion

Narrator

Narrator Long ago in a village on the side of a mountain there lived an old grandmother. Early one morning she set off with a basket of fruit.

Grandmother I'm going over the mountain to see my family.

(She walks round and round, pretending to climb the mountain. Wolf comes on.)

Wolf *(growling)* Ah, ha, here comes my breakfast! Get ready grandmother, I'm going to eat you.

Grandmother   Eat me? Eat me? Eat skinny old me? Oh no! You must wait till I come back from visiting my family on the other side of the mountain. My daughter's a very good cook and by then I'll be as fat as butter.

Wolf   *(feeling her arm)* You're right. You *are* skinny. I'll wait till you come back. Then I'll eat you.

(Wolf goes off and the grandmother keeps climbing.)

Grandmother   *(puffing)* Oh dear, here I am nearly at the top. I must have a rest. I'll sit near this rock while I catch my breath.

Narrator   But the rock was a tiger — a very hungry tiger.

Tiger   *(standing up)* Ah, ha, here's my morning tea! Get ready grandmother, I'm going to eat you.

Grandmother Eat me? Eat me? Eat skinny old me? Oh no! You must wait till I come back from visiting my family on the other side of the mountain. My daughter's a very good cook and by then I'll be as fat as butter.

Tiger *(feeling her arm)* You're right. You *are* skinny. I'll wait till you come back. Then I'll eat you.

(Tiger goes off and the grandmother keeps climbing.)

Grandmother *(puffing)* Well, here I am on top of the mountain. At least there's nothing here that wants to eat me.

(Lion jumps out from behind a rock.)

Lion That's what you think! I was wondering what I'd have for lunch. Get ready grandmother, I'm going to eat you.

Grandmother   Eat me? Eat me? Eat skinny old me? Oh, no! You must wait till I come back from visiting my family on the other side of the mountain. My daughter's a very good cook and by then I'll be as fat as butter.

Lion   *(feeling her arm)* You're right. You *are* skinny. I'll wait till you come back. Then I'll eat you.

(Lion goes off and the grandmother runs to the front of the stage.)

Grandmother   *(calling)* Daughter, son-in-law, grandchildren! Here I am, come to visit you from the other side of the mountain.

Narrator   One week later the grandmother decided to go back home. But first she asked her daughter to find a big butternut pumpkin. Then she cut a hole in the pumpkin big enough for her to crawl inside. Next morning she pushed the butternut pumpkin up to the top of the mountain.

Grandmother   *(puffing)* Well, here I am, on
top of the mountain again. Now all I have
to do is curl myself up into a ball and then
climb inside the butternut pumpkin.

(She does this.)

And off I roll
Bump, bump, bump
Down the mountain
Thump, thump, thump!

*(She tumbles over and
over. Lion pops up from
behind a rock.)*

Lion   What's this? What's this? A
talking pumpkin? Tell me pumpkin,
have you seen a fat old grandmother coming
over the mountain?

Grandmother   *(pretending to be a pumpkin)*
I saw some rocks
I saw a tree
But nothing else did I see.

Lion   She must be still at her
daughter's house,
eating and eating.
I'll go on waiting
here.

Grandmother *(still pretending to be a pumpkin)* Give me a push so I can roll down the mountain.

Lion   All right, pumpkin. Here you go!

(Lion gives the pumpkin a big push.)

Grandmother   And off I roll
Bump, bump, bump
Down the mountain
Thump, thump, thump!

(She tumbles over and over. Tiger pops up from behind a rock.)

Tiger   What's this? What's this? A talking pumpkin? Tell me pumpkin, have you seen a fat old grandmother coming down the mountain?

Grandmother *(still pretending to be a pumpkin)*
I saw a lion
near a tree
But nothing else did I see.

Tiger She must be still at her daughter's house, eating and eating. I'll go on waiting here.

Grandmother *(still pretending to be a pumpkin)* Give me a push so I can roll down the mountain.

Tiger All right, pumpkin. Here you go!

(Tiger gives the pumpkin a big push.)

Grandmother And off I roll
Bump, bump, bump
Down the mountain
Thump, thump, thump!

*(She tumbles over and over.
Wolf pops up from behind a rock.)*

Wolf   What's this? What's this? A talking pumpkin? Tell me pumpkin, have you seen a fat old grandmother coming down the mountain?

Grandmother   *(still pretending to be a pumpkin)*
A lion and tiger
near a tree
But nothing else did I see.

Wolf   I know that voice. It isn't a pumpkin voice. It's an old grandmother voice. A fat old grandmother voice!

(He picks up a stone and tries to break open the pumpkin.)

Narrator   The wolf hit the pumpkin with a stone and cracked it wide open. But quick as a flash, the grandmother jumped out just as the wolf jumped in.

Grandmother   I can hop as quick as a flea.
Silly old wolf
You won't catch me!

Narrator   And the wolf couldn't catch her because he was stuck fast in all the sticky squashed pumpkin inside the butternut pumpkin shell.

Wolf   Help! Help! I'm stuck in the pumpkin.

Grandmother   Serves you right, my foolish
friend! Wolves always come to a sticky
end.

(Then she walks off, saying:)

Grandmother   Snip, snap
Snip, snout
Now our story's
Quite told out.

Narrator   Off she went to have some tea.
And before the wolf got out of the
pumpkin, a hunter shot him stone dead.
As for the tiger and the lion – well,
they're still waiting, so don't go over the
mountain unless you're very skinny!

(The end)

Adapted from an Iranian folktale;
by *Pat Edwards*
illustrated by *Linda Forss*

What's AESOP'S STORY?

Who was Aesop?

Aesop, it's believed, was the author of "The Hare and the Tortoise" and other well known stories or fables. A fable is a short story that teaches a lesson. It usually has animals as the main characters and has a moral or message at the end.

Aesop was Greek and he lived in about 600 BC. It is thought that he was once a slave, but was given his freedom. No one knows where he was born, but he probably lived for a time in Athens.

Why do people still tell his stories?

Although Aesop lived long, long ago, the morals at the end of his fables are ones that can be used for people anywhere, any time.

The fable of the fox and the stork teaches that those who like playing jokes on other people must learn to laugh when a trick is played on them. And the story of the boy who cried "Wolf!" shows us that liars are not believed even when they do tell the truth.

Aesop's stories are always true. They help us think about the foolish things we all do and say sometimes.

Adapted from Aesop's fable,
The Hare and the Tortoise,
by Pat Edwards

Hi there, Slowcoach!

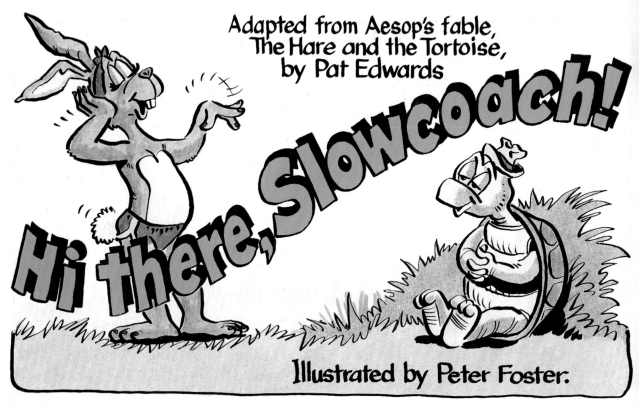

Illustrated by Peter Foster.

Once there was a hare and a tortoise.

Hi there, Hare!

Hi there, Slowcoach!

34

Animal stars ★★★★

★ This is Jody. She is a baby jaguar who was born on a farm in England. You don't often find wild animals on farms! Jody lives on a very special farm with many other animals that appear in the circus, on television, and in films.

★ Jody and the lion cub, called Pasha, are looked after by Sally Chipperfield. Her family have worked with animals for 300 years. Her father has a big circus and her Uncle Jimmy started safari parks. You drive through the parks and see the animals all around you.

Jody and Pasha have milk when they are babies. When they are a little bit older they eat minced meat, and later on they eat big joints of meat.

★ Sally's son, Jamie, is feeding raisins to the lemur. His name is Honeystripe, and as you can see he has a beautiful, long, striped tail.

★ Sally's husband is James Clubb. He trains the animals. He teaches them to do things they would do in the wild, like this big jump by Sonya the leopard. He works with them every day and gives them pieces of meat, saying 'Good boy' or 'Good girl' when they do the right thing.

★ James can pick up this leopard and carry her on his shoulders. Her name is Sascha. James works very closely with the animals. They are tame, but they can still be dangerous if they are upset. They have very sharp claws and teeth!

★ James watches the animals at play. Some are very good at jumping. This tiger went on her hind legs when playing and fighting, so James put this into the act.

Animal stars ★★★★

★ Today, James is working in a television film with two tigers, Delhi and Rajah. He and his helpers push the trailer into a big cage at the farm.

★ Delhi and Rajah come out of the trailer and look around. The television crew have put lots of trees in the ground so that it looks like a wood. In the film, the tigers have escaped from a safari park.

★ James pats Delhi before they start work. She is a very friendly tiger. Rajah is also very tame, but he is more rough when he plays.

★ Delhi runs round the bushes. James sends her the other way by tapping his two sticks. The television crew film just the tiger, which is what you see on the screen.

★ Buster is a Samoyed dog. Sally's friend Alexis is holding the hoop for him.

★ Here all the Samoyed dogs are pulling a sleigh bringing Father Christmas to a big store. The dogs also work in an act in the circus.

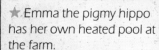
★ Emma the pigmy hippo has her own heated pool at the farm.

★ This is a dromedary, or Arabian camel. He has one hump.

Animal stars ★★★★

★ Zebras are wild horses from Africa. These ones are very tame and work with white mules in the circus.

★ The Arab horses do a 'liberty act' in the circus. It's called a liberty act because the horses are not ridden. The horses are also filmed for television advertisements. Each one has his own stall at the farm.

All the animals belonging to James and Sally were born in Great Britain. They have lots of each type of animal. This table tells you more about ten of those mentioned in this article.

Name	Animal	Food	Original country of the animal's parents or grandparents
Jody	jaguar	raw pork, fish	Central and South America
Pasha	lion	raw beef	Africa
Honeystripe	lemur	fruit, such as bananas and grapes	Madagascar
Sascha	leopard	raw chicken, rabbit	Africa and Asia
Delhi	tiger	raw beef	India
Buster	Samoyed dog	cooked meat, biscuits	Norway
Riad	Anglo-Arab horse	bran, hay, pony nuts	England
Zulie	zebra	bran, hay, pony nuts	South Africa
Soraya	Arabian camel	hay, bran, nuts	North Africa
Emma	pigmy hippopotamus	cabbages and other vegetables, bran, hay, pony nuts	Liberia

The Mouse War

Professor Branestawn was in a fix. His house in the town of Pagwell was being invaded by hundreds of mice. Every mousetrap he had set caught a mouse, and some had caught several. But the mice thought the traps were so nice that they were setting up house in them ...

They were sitting in little mice chairs, reading mice books and watching mice serials on miniature television sets.

"Oh my goodness!" cried Mrs Flittersnoop. "Instead of getting rid of our mice, these traps have attracted other people's!"

"I shall invent an anti-mouse powder," said the Professor. "They won't like the smell of it and they'll go away."
But the mice loved the anti-mouse powder. They not only thought it smelt nice, they thought it tasted nice too.

They had it for breakfast, dinner and supper. They even invented special recipes for using it.

But
oh dear!

Although the anti-mouse powder didn't get rid of
the mice, it turned them different colours.

There were now red-and-green-striped mice,
blue-spotted ones and ones with rainbow-
coloured patches.

"We must get cats!" cried the Professor rushing to the telephone

and falling over Mrs Flittersnoop's cat, who was cautiously studying a saucer of milk from all directions before drinking it.

The cats came in dozens and hundreds in reply to the Professor's appeal.

Cat lovers and cat homes sent them, and some boat
people even sent a catamaran, which was no use at all,
though they had meant to be helpful.

"Now we shall soon be rid of the mice," said the Professor.

"Yes, indeed, I do hope so, sir," said Mrs Flittersnoop.
But none of the cats had ever seen coloured, striped and
spotted mice before. They rather liked them. Some of the
motherly cats even let the mouse mothers out
of the traps to go for walks, while
they mouse-sat for them.

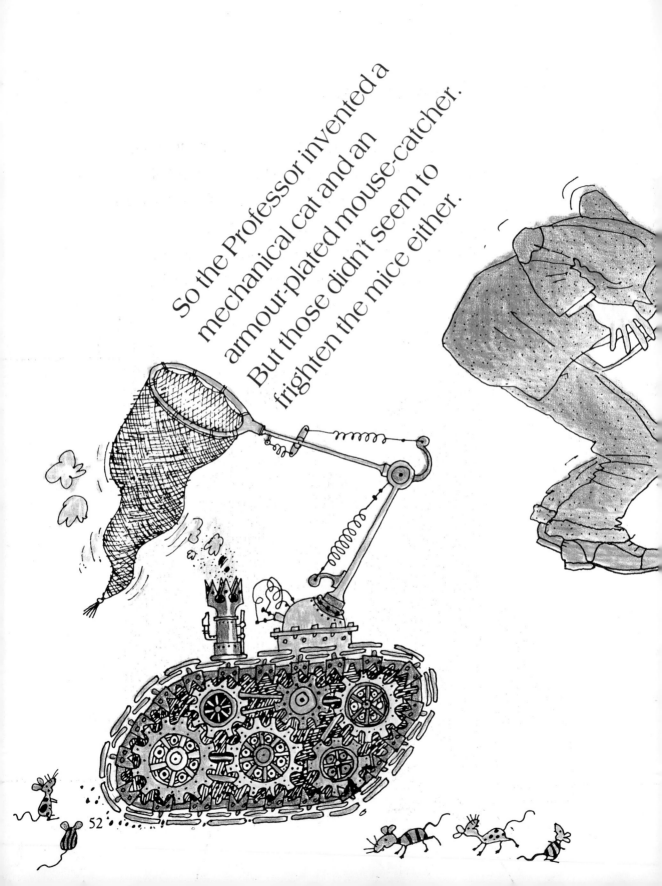

So the Professor invented a mechanical cat and an armour-plated mouse-catcher. But those didn't seem to frighten the mice either.

52

"Things are getting worse!"

cried the Professor as news came that the mice
were spreading through the Pagwell. A purple-
striped mouse got into Doctor Mumpzanmeazle's
surgery and stuck its tongue out at him.

Two spotted mice went shopping at Great
Pagwell Supermarket and scared the
customers.

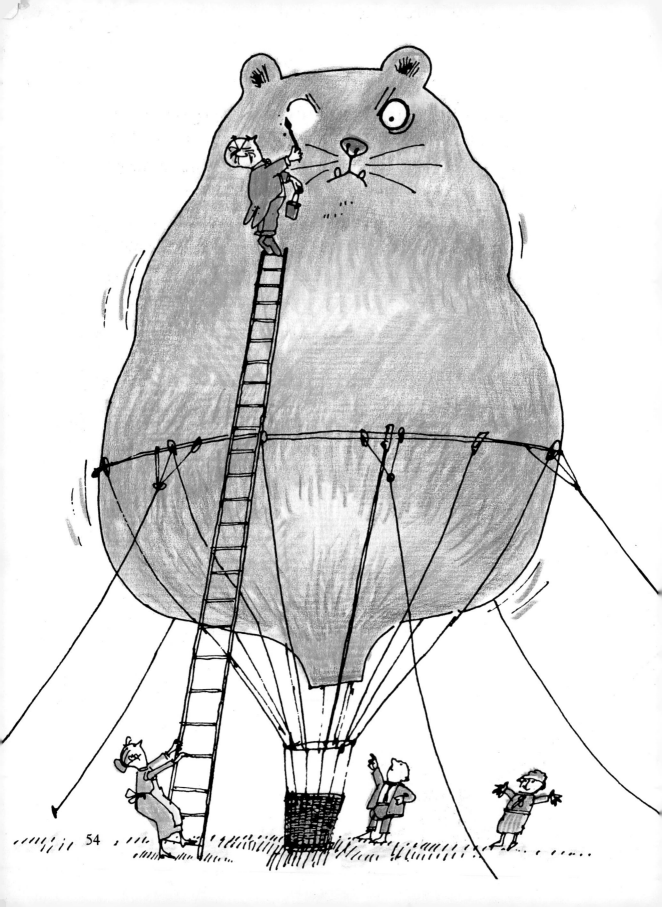

"If only I could blow up the mice without blowing up Pagwell," groaned the Professor. Then he clapped his hand to his head, missed and knocked off three pairs of spectacles.

"That's it!" he cried. "I shall blow up an enormous balloon in the shape of a terrifying cat. It will scare the mice, um, ah, away."

He persuaded the Pagwell Furnishing Company to give him the big plastic bags that they used to cover furniture. With help from friends and neighbours, he stuck these together so they formed one enormous bag which he blew up like a giant balloon. He tied a spare basket that he found at the Pagwell Laundry beneath it, and then painted a huge and frightening face of a cat on the balloon.

"Now!" cried the Professor, when the huge cat balloon was finished at last and ready to be launched. "Mice beware!" He jumped into the basket, the guy ropes were untied, and the balloon sailed upwards with all the people of Pagwell cheering below.

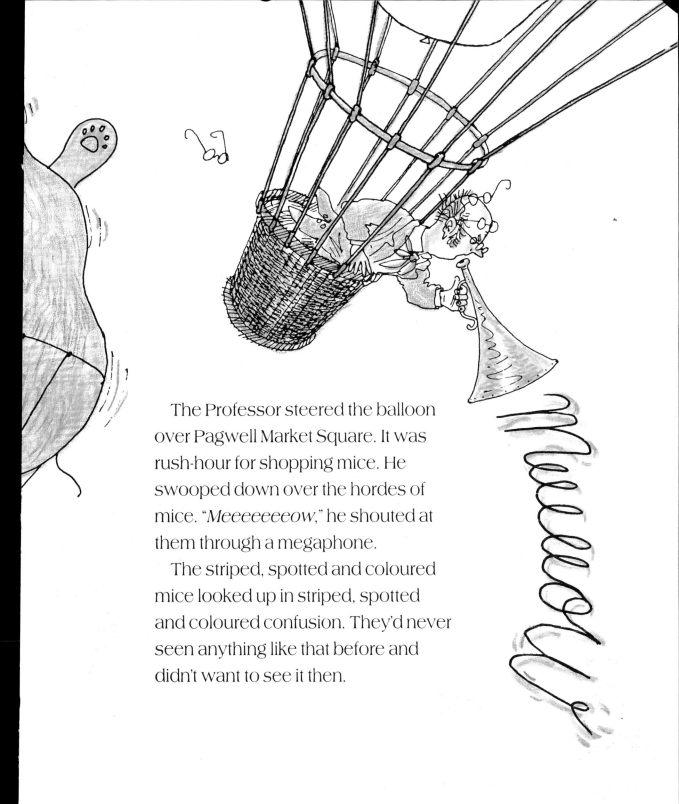

The Professor steered the balloon over Pagwell Market Square. It was rush-hour for shopping mice. He swooped down over the hordes of mice. "*Meeeeeeeow*," he shouted at them through a megaphone.

The striped, spotted and coloured mice looked up in striped, spotted and coloured confusion. They'd never seen anything like that before and didn't want to see it then.

Scamper scamper, rapetty rapetty, scratch, squeak, ow ow! They ran like the seven winds of goodness knows where. And after them went Professor Branestawm in his horrifying cat balloon.

Meeeeeow, grrrrr, hissss. Scampetty, scratch, squeak. The terrified striped, spotted and coloured mice rushed out of Pagwell. They poured through lanes, over meadows and  into the River Pag, which swept them away and they were never seen again.

Norman Hunter
illustrated by Gerald Rose

TIDDALIK

Tiddalik, the big green frog,

Spends all day sitting on a log.

In the mornings and the evenings too,

He likes to sing a little song to you,

He goes croak, croak, croak, croak,